HANSON

First published in 1997 by Virgin Books
an imprint of Virgin Publishing Ltd
332 Ladbroke Grove, London W10 5AH

A catalogue record for this book is available from the British Library

ISBN 0 7535 0169 4

Printed and bound by Butler & Tanner Ltd

Designed by Slatter-Anderson

HANSON

The Official Book by Jarrod Gollihare

Virgin

Introduction

Over the course of pop music history, few acts have grabbed the public attention like the pop rock band Hanson did in the spring of 1997. With the release of their first commercial single, 'MMMBop,' – which quickly shot to number one around the world – followed by the

huge success of their debut CD, *Middle of Nowhere*, Hanson became a fixture on pop radio throughout the summer of '97. In an 'MMMBop' it seemed, they were everywhere, appearing on popular television talk shows, gracing major magazines

with their exuberant charm, and, of course, always appearing on MTV – a virtual Hanson media explosion! Quite an amazing chain of events for a band whose members were aged 16, 14, and 11.

Which begs the question: What is it about these three blond brothers from Tulsa, Oklahoma, that has made them such a worldwide phenomenon in such a short

period of time? Is it their great harmonies? Their catchy melodies? Their fresh-faced charm? If you answered all of the above you're right on track.

Chapter One - The Early Years

Tulsa, Oklahoma, probably isn't the first place that springs to most people's minds when thinking of pop music. Though the city does have a surprisingly big music scene, and a rather rich rock 'n' roll and country music history, it is much more well-known for its oil and airplane industries than for the guitarists, pianists, and songwriters it has produced over the years.

Once known as the "Oil Capitol of the World" in the early part of the 20th century, Tulsa is now an affluent city of about 400,000 people. The story of Hanson begins in the rolling green hills of Tulsa's West Side. That's where Walker Hanson, an oil company manager, and his wife, Diana, raised their family of six children in a comfortable, semi-rural home.

Clarke Isaac (16), Jordan Taylor (14) and Zachary Walker (11) are the eldest of those kids, with sisters Jessica and Avery, and littlest brother Mackenzie comprising the younger half of the Hanson clan.

Weirdly enough, some people out there haven't quite fathomed Hanson's obvious family connection. If you implore Ike, Taylor or Zac to tell you about the silliest question posed to them during the past year they will laughingly recount a recent episode with a not-so-clever reporter who wanted to know, in all seriousness, how the band first met.

For the record, the Hanson boys are as brotherly as brotherly can be. This closeness is a direct result of their upbringing which included a firm sense of family and a belief in God. For Hanson, however, the good vibes of their lifestyles aren't a sales gimmick; their persona isn't an act. Ike, Taylor, and Zac are, simply put, genuine people.

Though the Hanson family calls Oklahoma home, they've moved around extensively due to Walker's job. They have lived for long periods in Washington, D.C., as well as Ecuador, Trinidad and Venezuela before finally settling back home in Tulsa. It was during this period of moving around that the boys discovered early rock 'n' roll.

"Nine years ago our dad started working for an oil company and within a year of getting the job

"People often assume the tapes were our parents' music that we just happened to listen to, actually, that music was before their time too!" Zac

the company asked him to go overseas," explains Ike. "Obviously, all of us weren't going to just stay at home, so we went with him."

"That was when we got these 50's and 60's tapes," continues Zac. "Our mom and dad got them before we left since there would be no English radio we could listen to where we were going. They were these 'Call now! Not available in stores!' type tapes. People often assume the tapes were our parents' music that we just happened to listen to. Actually that music was before their time, too! The three of us saw the TV commercial and asked them to buy them."

that of most of their peers. While kids back home in the States were getting into the 'alternative' and hip-hop lifestyles so common on '90s television and radio, the Hanson brothers were discovering their own musical heroes.

Otis Redding, Johnny Taylor, Chuck Berry, Aretha Franklin, The Supremes, The Temptations, The Four Tops, Buddy Holly, The Beatles, The Beach Boys, Elvis Presley – these were Hanson's musical mentors. "There's really nothing like that music," says Taylor. "It basically shaped pop music and everything you

"We got one of those tapes from 1958" explains Taylor "and it had songs like 'Johhny B. Good,' 'Splish Splash,' 'Rockin' Robin,' 'Summertime Blues,' and 'Good Golly Miss Molly' on it. There were tons of songs on there. We basically listened to that tape over and over and over until it really stuck in our heads."

This love for early rock 'n' roll, which intensified during the time they were living abroad, would give Ike, Taylor and Zac an early contact with popular music that was quite different from

hear now. That was the beginning of the rebellion of rock 'n' roll. Those guys are our heroes. Although we love what's on the radio now, that's the stuff that inspired us. That music is really kind of the basis of it all."

Little did any of them know how much of an influence all that early rock 'n' roll – with its emphasis on catchy melodies, short, concise songs, and, above all, a good beat – would have on the guys' growing creativity. They would soon begin to find out.

The story goes like this: There always was a lot of singing and music around the Hanson house. The guys would make up simple tunes to guitar at bedtime and they would sing around the table at mealtimes. At an early age, they definitely had an ear for harmony to the amazement of friends and relatives. Soon after, the three brothers began to improvise on their own around the house, working up the '50s and '60 rock and soul songs they'd come to love so much, complete with excellent harmonies, each brother singing a part. Even more impressively, it wasn't long before the boys began penning their own catchy songs.

"While we were overseas, was when Ike first started writing songs," says Taylor. "He wrote his first song, in Ecuador, on a small electric keyboard. The song was about the people on the streets; the poverty of where we were."

"We had a keyboard that we carried around with us," continues Ike. "I had just started learning how to play it. My mom showed me three chords on the keyboard, C, F, and G. So, with those chords we started writing songs. We went to private schools during that time – I was in third grade, Taylor was in first grade and Zac would have been, I guess, in kindergarten or pre-school."

"My mom showed me three chords on the keyboard, C, F, and G. So, with those chords we started writing songs" Ike

This earliest Hanson music, best described as sweet, soulful pop, revolved around everyday things like friends and family, the occasional love song, and their faith in God. Working with little more than their mini keyboard, their voices and their ideas, the boys began making "scrap tapes" – cassettes filled with musical ideas and "scrap pieces of songs" – eventually compiling a dozen or more of them. From these cassettes, the guys would go on to write around 100 songs over the next few years.

Upon settling back home in Tulsa after their travels, it was decided that Diana would teach her kids at home, a decision that would ultimately prove very helpful to Hanson's musical development. "Our mom wanted to home school us because she wanted to have a closer relationship with us," says Zac, who points out that home schooling is quite popular in Tulsa. Indeed, this not only gave the guys much more quality time with their parents, but with each other as well, acting as a greenhouse of sorts for the boys' growing musical abilities. All that extra time together allowed Ike, Taylor, and Zac to develop their singing abilities and hone their songwriting skills.

In 1992, The Hanson Brothers, as they were then called, made their debut public performance at a large music and arts festival called Mayfest held annually in downtown Tulsa. With the promise of summer thick in the air and the afternoon sun glinting off the high rise buildings and lighting up the tents set-up throughout the streets, Mayfest was the perfect setting for The Hanson Brothers' introduction to the general public. Performing a 30-minute a cappella (unaccompanied) set, the boys wowed the audience with their exuberance, charm, and great harmonies.

Not long afterward, they began receiving offers to sing at parties, corporate functions, festivals, amusement parks, and sporting events. Offers from nightclubs weren't forthcoming, however, due in part to their ages (most clubs in Oklahoma are 21-and-over establishments) and the nature of their music – not exactly rock, clearly not blues, and definitely not country. None of that mattered, however, as The Hanson Brothers' schedule began filling up quite nicely without club bookings.

It would be the decision to begin booking the band at local schools for student assemblies that would lead to the first real glimpses of the fame to come. A couple of teachers who saw a performance or two elsewhere suggested that the brothers bring the show to their students.

The idea was to use Hanson's performance to show their students what they could accomplish if they focused on their own aims and goals. It was during these performances that the initial tremblings of Hansonmania were felt.

Zac

"We would make up simple tunes to guitar and sing around the table."

"We're three guys who write, play and sing our music... That's what Hanson is."
Taylor

Hanson, as they came to be called in 1993, began developing a decidedly more modern sound. What began as a 'doo-wop' threesome singing cover songs written well before they were ever born, was quickly developing into a 'rhythm and blues' influenced sound, which included pop hits, as well as their own songs, in their set.

Life around the Hanson home had become busier and busier for Ike, Taylor, and Zac during this period. All three brothers began piano lessons with Donald Ryan, an accomplished classical pianist. And when not practicing, studying, playing sports, or performing, the boys started taking dance lessons under the direction of Ja'Marc Davis, a local dancer. Ja'Marc became a close friend and an important source of encouragement over the next few years.

A decision was made to take the furniture out of the living room and convert it into a practice space complete with a giant mirror along one wall so the boys could check out their performances during rehearsals. As Ike put it in an interview with Urban Tulsa magazine during that period, "We want to be a Boyz II Men/Ace of Base type group where we can sing harmony and dance."

And dance they did. Singing to pre-recorded tracks (most of which they produced themselves), Hanson's live performances became high energy, hip-hop dance and harmony specials.

At this point in their career, Ike and Taylor played some of their songs live on the keyboard, other tracks Ike programmed himself which the three of them could dance to. Over the course of time, several other musicians produced Hanson's songs as well. At every

"There was an outdoor barbecue going on and all these industry people were there. We would just walk up to them and say 'Can we sing for you?'" Taylor

"I was having lunch in Austin when the guys came up to me and asked if they could sing for me. They sang a cappella and I just said, 'Where are your parents? I need to talk to them fast." Christopher Sabec (manager)

"We wanted to be a Boyz II Men/Ace of Base type group where we can sing harmony and dance." Ike

Their goal was simple: sing for whoever would listen.

performance, however, the brothers included some a cappella numbers in their set; this was where they started out musically and they still loved to break into a cappella harmony.

It was about this time that the kids at Hanson's public school performances began to go absolutely mad for them. Girls (and women) would scream. Young fans would proclaim, teary-eyed, the name of their best-loved Hanson. Yammering teen and pre-teen fans would call the family's home and squeal 'I love you' into the answering machine. Ike, Taylor, and Zac began to be recognized in public places and approached for autographs. Pretty heady stuff for a trio of guys who were not old enough to date girls. The boys took it all in their stride: "You can't help liking it," said Taylor at the time. "But some of them are just so fanatical, and they scream so much you just can't talk to them," added Ike.

In March of 1994, Hanson took a trip to Austin, Texas, to attend South by Southwest, a major music conference that annually draws hundreds of music industry executives and thousands of hopeful musicians to the Lone Star State for a week of lectures and concerts. Their goal was simple: sing for whoever would listen. It quickly became obvious that this was no easy task. "We got there on the last day," says Taylor. "There was an outdoor barbecue going on and all these industry people were there. We would just walk up to them and say 'Can we sing for you?' Some of them would push us away and say 'Sorry,' and some of them listened, but just kind of blew us off."

Indeed, looking back, the scene must have seemed really strange. Here, at the very peak of grunge's popularity were three well-scrubbed, blond lads running about, singing a cappella pop songs to a bunch of record company people who were looking to discover the next Pearl Jam, not the next Jackson 5.

As fate would have it, their path crossed with a young entertainment lawyer named Christopher Sabec who was in town for the conference and at the time was representing the Dave Matthews Band. An unabashed music fan and Grateful Dead fanatic, Sabec was looking for something different but he wasn't sure what.

"We sang for him and he liked it," says Taylor. "Then he walked with us over to where we had a stereo set up and we sang and danced to a track we had of one of our songs. After that he was really interested."

As Sabec said to a journalist, "I was having lunch in Austin when the guys came up to me and asked if they could sing for me. Everyone else was ignoring them. They sang a cappella and I just said, 'Where are your parents? I need to talk to them fast!'"

This proved to be a major step forward in Hanson's climb toward a record deal. Sabec left Austin the next day with their telephone number, and his head full of their perfectly harmonized melodies. Hanson returned home to Tulsa with memories of a great Texas barbecue, but no firm interest from record companies as yet.

What the band did have was some vital help from the experienced Jim Halsey, music industry agent and long-time manager of country singer Roy Clark. The band met Jim at a music industry seminar, Jim gave them some important guidance and introduced the guys to Bill Coben, a music attorney who had also worked with Roy Clark. Bill proved to be a great help for Hanson in negotiating and eventually rejecting an early offer from a big record company. From his experience with recording contracts and industry know-how, Bill traded draft contracts with the interested company. When he had

exhausted all options, he gave the band some advice: in his opinion, the contract being offered was not one the band could feel good about. In fact, he told them, "If the band is successful, you will hate yourself for signing this". Consequently, Hanson said no to this first, and at the time, only offer on the table. The band, however, was not discouraged. On the contrary, they were in no hurry to rush into anything and were confident they had made the right decision. With ever-increasing demands from Tulsa fans to release a record, it soon became apparent that Hanson needed to record an album. So in the Autumn of 1994, the band booked some studio time and cut their first album, *Boomerang*, recording in both Nashville and Chicago.

Boomerang is a perfect example of the band's earliest music. Pop R&B songs abound throughout, from the catchy, crowd-pleasing title track to the ballad, 'More Than Anything,' to the a cappella groove of 'Rain.' Six of the nine tracks were written by the boys, with three cover songs rounding it out, including a revved-up version of the old Coasters hit, 'Poison Ivy,' and a dead-on take of The Jackson 5's 'The Love You Save.'

Boomerang's most endearing quality for many fans is that it is music written and performed by young, talented, and joyful artists who couldn't care less about what the music critics of the world thought of them. Although the music on *Boomerang* has a much more synthetic feel than their next two releases, it doesn't affect the obvious sincerity in the guys' singing. And it doesn't change the fact that these catchy songs were written by boys who were, amazingly enough, 13, 10 and 8 years old at the time. Strangely, the CD cover that goes with the *Boomerang* disc is a globe: in a few more years, Hanson would be taking that globe by storm.

"Because of the video we did, we actually got interest from a record company who then heard *Boomerang* and wanted to hear even more of our stuff." Isaac

Shortly after *Boomerang*'s release, and about a year after they attended South by Southwest, the Hanson family received a call from Christopher Sabec. "He was coming through on a plane and Tulsa was right in the middle of where he was going," says Taylor. "So, he remembered us and said, 'What the heck? I'll stop for a day and see what's up with these guys.'" Christopher arrived in Tulsa the next day in time to catch the end of a performance at a mall and see first hand the response of the local fans. He ended up staying with the family for two weeks and by the end of his visit, they had taken him on as their manager.

By June of 1995, Hanson had performed more than 300 times in public. They were becoming seasoned performers well-known for their exciting performances, and with the release and success of *Boomerang*, people other than local pop lovers were beginning to take notice of them. With Christopher tirelessly touting Hanson around New York and Los Angeles as 'the next big thing,' it would surely be just a matter of time before record companies began making offers. But, as with so many bands , which eventually go on to success,the going at first was not easy. "Christopher shopped *Boomerang* around to different labels and we got some interest, but nothing really clicked," says Isaac. "In fact, we were even flown to Los Angeles by a record label to audition, but nothing ever really materialized."

Indeed, Christopher was having a hard time convincing his colleagues and label executives to take his new clients seriously. Hanson, he was told over and over again, was a dead end, an act to be dropped quickly to avoid humiliation. "I had friends telling me 'Dude don't do it – don't embarrass yourself,'" Sabec informed *Entertainment Weekly*. Much to his frustration, the record company rejection slips began to pile up.

Back in Tulsa, however, the Hansons remained unconcerned. Patience definitely rules the roost at the Hanson home, and Walker and Diana – not your usual 'showbiz parents' eager to sign away their kids' lives – were content to let their sons' musical careers take off at whatever pace was necessary, however slow that might be. Ike, Taylor, and Zac (themselves quite level-headed about the foibles and pitfalls of the music industry) were equally patient. Although the guys could think of nothing that they'd rather be doing than making music for a living, the limelight would just have to wait.

It was around this time that Hanson's sound began to change yet again. The guys' personal

"While we were working on background vocals for 'Lonely Boy'

during the *Boomerang* recording we

came up with the chorus for 'MMMBop.'

Taylor

It was a rougher version, but the bulk

of it was there."

tastes in music had begun to swing away from the slick Top 40 R&B-hip-hop with which they had had so much local success in the past few years. They were getting into rock-style pop these days – less Ace of Base and Boyz II Men, more Spin Doctors, Aerosmith, and Counting Crows – and with that change came a desire to play as a band. After investing in a cheap guitar, electronic keyboards, and borrowing a Beatles-style Ludwig drum kit from a friend who had it stored in an attic, the guys dived headlong into the tough job of becoming a rock 'n' roll band. Ike moved from the keyboards to the guitar, the ultra-active Zac was naturally drawn to the energy of the drums, and Taylor, who at first split his time between keyboards and drums, eventually settled on the former. The family living room became more than just a dance rehearsal space. Soon it was a practice hall as well, with the sounds of guitar riffs and drum rolls filling the air of many an afternoon after they had finished their school work.

In September of 1995, Hanson put together a video of themselves in order to audition for a soft drink commercial. "We got together with a local director that we knew and his small crew, and we put together a little music track with another friend and did this whole music video,"

'Oh, man that sounds really cool!' **Ike**

says Taylor. The video impressed the soft drink company, Hanson won the part, and they were subsequently flown to Los Angeles to film the commercial. Although it was eventually scrapped without being aired, the experience opened some doors for the band. "It was sort of a blessing in disguise, I guess," says Isaac. "Because of the video we did, we actually got interest from a record company who then heard

Boomerang and wanted to hear even more of our stuff. They said 'Hey guys, could you do some demos (low budget recordings) for us?'" Those demos were the catalyst for Hanson's second CD, *MMMBop*. Although the record label's interest in Hanson eventually stalled when the company experienced a re-organization, the band mixed together the new demos they had made for the label and added more tunes, to come up with a whopping 15-song album. Recorded in late 1995 at Louis Drapp Studio and Natura Studio in Tulsa, then mixed at Sound of Music in Richmond, Virginia, *MMMBop* gave the guys a chance to really show off their growing songwriting and playing skills. "We composed all the songs and played pretty much every instrument," says Ike, "except for bass. We did most of the recording in this guy's garage studio, and he was a bass player, so he ended up playing it on several of the songs."

Interestingly, *MMMBop* contains early versions of 'Thinking of You,' 'With You In Your Dreams,' and, you guessed it, 'MMMBop' the single, that would later appear on Hanson's major label debut, *Middle of Nowhere*. Though this early version of 'MMMBop' is much slower and not as groovy as the later version which would go on to become a worldwide smash hit, it still stands out as a great pop song, worthy of its place in the records of popular music. As

Christopher Sabec notes, "When I listen to the demo I shopped of 'MMMBop' that the guys did on their own, there's no question that all the elements to the song are there. The melody, the chorus, the arrangement it's all there. I'll always be puzzled why so many labels missed the hit-song potential of that demo."

The ultra-catchy chorus for 'MMMBop,' originally conceived during the recording of *Boomerang*, had been with the guys for over a year before they finished the song. "While we were working on background vocals for 'Lonely Boy' during the *Boomerang* recording we came up with the chorus for 'MMMBop,'" says Taylor. "It was a rougher version, but the bulk of it came up. We had that in our ears and our heads for a while and then about a year later, basically out of the blue, we came up with the verses and the 'Can you tell me?' section, and it became more of a structured song. So over about a period of a year we wrote the full song."

"Yeah," continues Ike, "I can often remember times we would be walking around the house and we would go, 'Oh, remember that background part from the album? Let's sing that.' Then we would go into it and we'd be like, 'Oh, man that sounds really cool.' As time went on it became its own thing – it took on a life of its own."

An 'MMMBop,' in case you don't already

"I got this tape and I loved it – but I was convinced it was a fake. I thought that maybe they had been manufactured. I was sure there was some adult pulling the strings, or the vocals were manipulated, or they weren't really playing their instruments. " Steve Greenberg on Hanson

'Cherish your friends and loved ones now, for in an instant they may be gone.'

know, is a measurement of time, like a moment or an instant, according to Ike. The song's simple and deep meaning is this: Cherish your friends and loved ones now, for in an instant they may be gone. Wise words indeed from such young souls.

It was around this time that Hanson began performing at the only club in Tulsa that can lay claim to booking the trio way back when: The Blue Rose Café. Owner Tom Dittus, an acquaintance of the Hanson family, recognized the boys' talents early on and believed they had a broader public appeal than simply with kids. Though his club, located in Tulsa's hip Brookside district, usually featured bluesy rock bands playing for an adult audience, Dittus decided to take a chance on the boys. He was not disappointed.

Because of their ages, Ike, Taylor and Zac couldn't set foot inside the 21-and-over establishment, but they could set-up in the parking lot next to the popular Blue Rose patio – as many bands do during the spring and summer seasons – and blast away to their hearts' content. And so they did. Hanson made several appearances over the next few months, drawing not only their own ever-growing crowd (who had to sit in the parking lot as well, of course) and their parents, but also substantial interest from other customers.

One of those customers, Mark Carr, a local musician himself and another friend of the Hanson family, recalls the Blue Rose performances fondly. "At that time they hadn't been playing their instruments for too long," he says, "but I could tell they'd come a long way. They'd really been practicing a lot."

Carr chuckles when he recalls the boys' stage antics, though. "Zac would make all sorts of

strange noises between songs. He looked like he wanted to jump up from behind his drum kit, run off, and do something else. And Ike would start playing that Stone Temple Pilots tune, 'Interstate Love Song,' between each song. The girls up front would squeal every time he did it."

As it turns out, however, the girls squealed for pretty much the entire show. "The response even then with the local kids was almost as impressive as what I see nowadays on television. Hanson's fans thought the band were stars even then. They were yelling and screaming frantically. It was pretty surreal."

Hanson made *MMMBop* available for the first time to the Tulsa public at their annual Mayfest performance in 1996. The fan response was, to put it mildly, highly receptive. Halfway across the country in Los Angeles, Christopher Sabec sensed the beginnings of a better reception at the record companies and he began sending out demos from *MMMBop*. In fact, interest in Hanson began to grow rapidly as many A&R (Artists and Repertoire) departments – the folks in charge of signing new talent – began to notice a steady decline in the popularity of depressing rock and gangster rap. Something was definitely changing and cautious record companies began talking about finding "the next big thing."

In the midst of such uncertainty in the music industry, Christopher began getting signs of interest from various labels and by the spring of '96, he had his hands full, wheeling and dealing with many potentially interested parties. Despite all the telephone calls and conversations,

'Hanson's fans

It was pretty surreal.' Mark Carr

however, nothing clicked. When the demo fell into the hands of Mercury Records West Coast General Manager Allison Hamamura and President and Chief Executive Officer Danny Goldberg, however, sparks began to fly. They passed the tape on to Steve Greenberg, a pop expert at the label and currently senior vice president and head of A&R for Mercury in New York. Greenberg was hooked immediately. He had his doubts as well, though. As he told *The New York Times*, "I got this tape and I loved it – but I was convinced it was a fake. I thought maybe they had been manufactured. I was sure there was some adult pulling the strings, or the vocals were manipulated, or they were not really playing their instruments." Greenberg notes "A lot of A&R departments are worried about their own image if they sign a teen act."

To calm his fears, Christopher invited Greenberg to make a trip to Coffeyville, Kansas, in April of 1996 where Hanson was performing at a local fair in order to check the boys out himself. "He came to one of our least responsive shows," moans Ike. "I mean, we performed well, but the audience didn't really get into it." Taylor continues: "It was one of those shows where you go 'Why did he have to come to this show?' Afterwards, we all drove back to our house in Tulsa, which I guess took about an hour. We threw a football around in the back and just talked to him a little bit. Later, he told us 'You know, basically I was coming out here to see

what was wrong with you guys. Either you didn't write songs, you didn't sing, or you didn't play.' He was sure that something wasn't going to be what it was on our album."

"That night," Ike resumes, "we sat down on the couch, everybody, Christopher and all of us, and we talked to Steve about his ideas and things like that. He ended up not leaving until the next morning."

"And we really thought after that we would never see him again," says Taylor, jumping back in, "because he left and said 'You know, if this never happens, I just wish you guys luck in the future and I really hope you guys do well.' He kind of left it sounding like we were never going to see him again." They were mistaken.

The Coffeyville performance had really wowed Greenberg, despite the band's views on the performance. "They sang as well as they sang on the record, and played as well as they played on the record," says Greenberg. "I was surprised on both counts." That performance, combined with the short time he spent with Isaac, Taylor, and Zac had cemented one fact: These were real musicians with real charm – a rare combination of talents. Within a month, Hanson would be signed to Mercury, who would declare them one of their top acts. Thus, just two months after the release of their second self-produced album, the search for a record deal was over. The band was heading out to Los Angeles to record their next album – big things were about to happen.

Chapter Five- California Dreaming

Hanson seemed to be charting a new course for popular music and Mercury had signed on for the gamble. Top-notch producers were sought out. As a result, the Dust Brothers (the duo of John King and Michael Simpson who had produced Beck's megahit, Grammy Award-winning *Odelay*, and the Beastie Boys acclaimed *Paul's Boutique*) and Steve Lironi (who has worked with notable British acts Black Grape and Space) were hired to man the recording consoles. Hanson would end up spending five months writing and recording *Middle of Nowhere* in Los Angeles, from July until November 1996.

In the same way that Walker's former job with the oil company caused the entire family to relocate for a long period of time years back, so now would his three eldest sons' career mean yet another temporary move for the family. Only this time it would be to a house in the beautiful Hollywood Hills.

"You could actually see the Hollywood sign from the deck on the back of the house," says Ike. "And you could see Mann's Chinese Theater, too."

"You could look down at night and there was this awesome view of the city," recalls Taylor. "You could walk to Runyon canyon and you could see everything, I mean, it would blow you away."

The guys also really liked the wildlife in the area. Everything from coyotes to wild deer to foxes to rather large snakes could be found on or about their property at one point or another during their several months' stay.

"Who knows what wildlife was living in our backyard?" quips Taylor. "Who would think you could be in the middle of Los Angeles and have coyotes running across your back patio," says Taylor.

Several well-known songwriters heard samples of Hanson's earlier writing and agreed to co-write with Hanson. While the label had a great deal of respect for Ike, Taylor, and Zac's songwriting abilities – for example, 'MMMBop,' composed solely by the boys, was the first single released – Greenberg felt that the band would benefit from working and writing with experienced professionals.

The list of songwriters that agreed to write with Hanson is truly impressive: The legendary

Ike

"You could

actually see the

Hollywood

sign from the

deck on the back

of the house"

"Think about how many times you say 'weird'" Taylor

The most important thing to me was

Mark Hudson on Isaac

Cynthia Weil and Barry Mann worked with the boys on the ballad 'I Will Come For You.' They are best known for the smash hit 'You've Lost that Lovin' Feeling' originally penned for The Righteous Brothers, as well as scores of other hits for other artists such as The Animals and The Crystals.

Ellen Shipley, joined Ike, Taylor, and Zac to pen the song 'Yearbook,' an ode to a missing classmate.

Ellen is best known for the Belinda Carlisle hits 'Heaven is a Place on Earth' and 'Circle in the Sand.'

Desmond Child, whose credits include work with Bon Jovi and Aerosmith, worked with Hanson on the emotional ballad 'Weird.' About the writing of this song, Taylor recalls, "We were talking about the fact that nobody had ever written a song about the word 'weird.' It seemed strange to us. Think about how many times you say 'weird.'" (Well, at least the three members of Hanson say it a lot – it is definitely one of their most-used words!) Ike continues, "We said let's try that and Desmond sat down at the keyboard and we just started doing melodies and lyrics. That one came together quickly. It was very much a mood thing."

The songwriter responsible for four of the joint efforts, was Mark Hudson.

Well-known in the '70s as a member of The Hudson Brothers, another trio of singing siblings, as well as the co-host of The Hudson Brothers' variety show on CBS, Mark has enjoyed a career as both a hit-making pop musician and a TV personality. Nowadays, he is very much in demand as a songwriter. His past credits include 'Livin' On The Edge' with Aerosmith, among many other hits.

With Hanson, Mark worked on three songs: 'Where's The Love,' 'Lucy,' and 'A Minute Without You'.

"For 'A Minute Without You,' we had written just about all of the song and then (Mark Hudson) finished it off," says Taylor. Hudson agrees that his addition to the song was minimal. "This was their song," he says. "They brought it to me, only what they thought was the 'bridge' (the link between choruses) was in fact the chorus. I tinkered with it musically. The most important thing to me was that it be Isaac's song. Isaac's got a great voice."

Writing *Middle of Nowhere* was a completely new experience for Ike, Taylor, and Zac. For years, they had been a complete songwriting

"A lot of the time what happens when you're working with other songwriters is you both bring ideas for songs and you work on either one or both your ideas." Taylor

unit, relying on nobody but themselves for lyrics, melodies, and arrangements. Suddenly, they found themselves working with famous, experienced songsmiths on a daily basis. It was an amazing opportunity for the three of them.

"It was weird at first," explains Ike, "because we were learning how to work with other people and learning how to exchange ideas."

"And not irritate each other," continues Taylor.

"Of course, we were thinking at first, 'Well, this is kind of odd; why would we want to write with somebody else?' chimes in Zac. But we actually had great experiences with everybody. It was cool because we wrote with some incredible people. "We were amazed", continues Taylor,"that such well-known writers were willing to write with an unknown band on their debut record.""I think we made a good album,"added Zac

Indeed, they did make a good album, as public response and critical praise eventually showed. The music on *Middle of Nowhere* benefits from the creative give and take that took place naturally when you combine seasoned songwriters with the fresh musical ideas and songwriting ability of Hanson.

"A lot of the time what happens when you're working with other songwriters is you both bring ideas for songs and you work on either one or both your ideas," says Taylor. "And sometimes that would make another song come about."

"For example, what we were doing with Mark Hudson, really in a lot of ways, was very similar to the way we were used to writing," says Ike. "We would sit there together in his studio where he has at least 25 guitars hanging on his walls. Ike would grab a guitar, Taylor would go to the B3 organ, we'd set up some drums and we would jam on songs."

Hanson's second single, 'Where's the Love?' definitely went through some changes before it finally settled into its own groove.

"The song started out with more of a disco feel. As we worked on the song it took on some minor elements. Then we threw on some beefier drums and slightly more distorted guitar. That totally altered the feel of it."

"That's an example of the back and forth nature of writing with someone," says Ike. "The song has a rock 'n' roll feel, but it's also got a Motown feel, too."

"If everybody liked it, it would be on the album." *Zac*

The process of song selection for *Middle of Nowhere* went like this: after the guys finished working up a new song, they would make a quick demo of the song and submit it to Mercury. "If everybody liked it, it would be on the album," explains Zac.

"We ended up submitting more than 36 songs," says Taylor. "We thought that was a lot, but apparently other groups present up to 60 songs sometimes. So you see, it's amazing how many songs get presented, but..." "So little get used," chips in Zac.

Another dynamic part of recording *Middle of*

Nowhere was working with the ultra-hip Dust Brothers. "They were really cool to work with," recalls Ike. "The whole vibe of the studio was very laid back. We'd come to the studio about noon, sit down, and talk a little while and when we felt like starting we would. They have a great record collection, obviously, 'cause they use a lot of different sampled things. So they'd play us different records, like Three Dog Night or something by The Pointer Sisters and they have all the Beatles records. It was really cool."

"The Dust Brothers have a very different style to most producers," explains Taylor, "because they

"The whole vibe of the studio was very laid back. We'd come to the studio about noon, sit down, and talk a little while and when we felt like starting we would. They have a great record collection, obviously, 'cause they use a lot of different sampled things. So they'd play us different records, like Three Dog Night or The Pointer Sisters and they have all the Beatles records too." Ike on Dust Brothers

just basically work out of a house, recording drums and vocals in the living room. In one of the bedrooms, they have the mixing board and their computer and all of the recording equipment. We would also have the keyboards or the bass in the bedroom, but they would put the guitar amplifiers in the hall. It's just a different style from what you would expect. By the way, their living room is where we did the 'MMMBop' video."

The Dust Brothers definitely left their mark on Hanson's groovy pop sound, says Ike, but it's not over-the-top. "They didn't radically change our sound, but they added some interesting things that we might not have thought of. 'MMMBop' is a good example. They added a 'ruh-uh-ruh-uh-ruh' scratch thing. But that's really all the scratching that's on the album."

"I think what the Dust Brothers and Stephen Lironi brought back to our sound," says Taylor, "was a little of the R&B – with all the 'loops' and scratches and sampled sounds – combined with pop rock."

Interestingly, work on *Middle of Nowhere* took place in five studios. "It was kind of a weird process," says Taylor, "because sometimes we would do some vocal parts in one studio and then Stephen Lironi would have some of his equipment set up in another and we would run back and forth between studios, doing vocals in one and recording instruments in the other. Then we'd have another studio where we'd be recording a string section. It was very crazy."

What happened in all five recording studios at

that time was pure magic – one of those rare instances when the right artists are combined with the right producers with the right songs under the right circumstances, and the music that is created touches a nerve that goes beyond everyone's best hopes.

After visiting Los Angeles at one point during the recording process Steve Greenberg flew back to New York with a new mix of 'MMMBop.' He was blown away by what he heard there.

"When Steve was working on 'MMMBop' and first brought it to the office I would hear it between five and 25 times a day," says David Silver, Senior Vice President at Mercury whose office happened to be right next to Greenberg's. "He just kept playing it over and over again. I never got sick of hearing it, though. It's an amazing song. Just in the same way I still love to hear 'All Shook Up,' by Elvis Presley or 'Blueberry Hill,' by Fats Domino, I still love hearing 'MMMBop.' It's a bit eerie, it's so good."

While living in the Hollywood Hills wasn't exactly tough for Ike, Taylor, and Zac – after five months of recording thousands of miles from home, they were quite ready to head back to Oklahoma for a break and a chance to see their friends. "We definitely missed home," said Ike in a recent interview. "But we've gone back to L.A. many times."

"And it really does feel like a home away from home now," finished Taylor.

Their visit to Tulsa didn't last too long, though. In March of '97, they were required back in Los Angeles to shoot a video for 'MMMBop,' the

single chosen to introduce Hanson to the world. To direct the video, the band chose Tamra Davis, whose resumé included the Adam Sandler film Billy Madison, as well as music videos for Sonic Youth, Veruca Salt, and Luscious Jackson.

The guys were very much a part of the decision-making process for both who would direct the 'clip' and what it would be about. "To begin with, we watched Tamra Davis' videos and kinda reviewed what she'd done," says Taylor. "Then, later, we were in New York doing some

press and promotion, and we talked with her. We didn't know what to expect, but we started throwing ideas back and forth and we really hit it off because she was so open and receptive to our ideas."

"We all really just clicked," says Ike. "We felt really comfortable talking to her."

"We brought up this idea of using shots of the moon," continues Taylor. "We had thought about the future and the past. Like 'In an MMMBop they're gone,' and you go to the past...'In an MMMBop they're not there' and you're in the future on the moon"

When we brought up the moon she said "She had just been watching some footage of the old Apollo missions," injects Ike. "It was just a weird coincidence. That was one of the things that clicked between us, though."

The video was shot over the course of two days in Los Angeles, much of it in front of either a "green screen" onto which various scenes were projected, or in front of a large fabric flower. (The guys now have that flower tacked up on one of the walls in their garage practice space at home in Tulsa.) Other shots of the guys running about at the beach, pretending to drive a car (which was actually being towed in a park in Los Angeles), rollerblading in a parking lot,

and performing in the Dust Bothers' living room fill-out the video.

The rollerblading shots almost didn't happen, however. "We had maybe 20 minutes of daylight left," says Ike. "We drove to kind of a mall area, I guess you'd call it. What do you call those?"

"A strip center," says Zac. "It just happened that the cameraman knew how to skateboard."

"So the cameraman got on a skateboard and held the camera and just followed us around," continues Ike. "There was an accident, which is the very last thing that happened, where the cameraman was on his skateboard in the middle of the parking lot and I was way off to another side ."

Taylor takes up the story from here. "Zac and I were just rollerblading around and we both looked back to see the camera. Right before we looked forward again, we suddenly collided. The cameraman just barely missed us, but he happened to get that shot. It was kind of like a weird coincidence that happened to really work."

With filming of the 'MMMBop' video wrapped-up, Hanson headed back home to Tulsa for a few weeks to relax and practise their live show in a small rented theater. It would prove to be the guys' last few weeks of relative anonymity: once released, 'MMMBop' would change their lives forever.

"I still love hearing 'MMMBop.' It's a bit eerie, it's so good."

David Silver on 'MMM'Bop'

Nothing prepared Hanson for the response 'MMMBop' received from the public when it was released to American radio in March 1997. At best, Ike, Taylor, and Zac figured they had a decent chance of getting a hit with their debut single, given the catchiness of the song, the quality of the recording and their performances, and the promotional push given by Mercury. No one, however, could have predicted the hysteria that was about to erupt. 'MMMBop' debuted at Number 43 on Billboard's Airplay chart, a measurement of how often a song is played on American radio stations nationwide. By early June, it would hit number one in Hanson's homeland.

To add to the excitement, MTV began broadcasting the 'MMMBop' video almost immediately after its release in March. It was an instant smash, rocketing up the US charts to Number 1. In addition, the video got lots of airplay on VH-1 and The Box in America, and Canada's Much Music and Music Plus. For the record, MTV was an early supporter of Hanson and their music. In fact, MTV was so sure of Hanson's potential, that in February – well before the song was released, let alone a hit – they invited the guys to tape a live performance of 'MMMBop' for an episode of The Jenny McCarthy Show (a popular show) that wouldn't be aired until June.

"It was kind of cool because the audience at the show really did not know who we were," says Ike. "They had no clue because the song hadn't even really hit. It was just kind of building up momentum."

"They were looking for some band they would know," says Taylor, "maybe some alternative group. So it was kind of a weird thing, but we started interacting with the crowd in between takes, clapping and goofing around, and just made it really fun."

In addition, 'MMMBop' did really well in the sales charts. In May, it entered Billboard's Hot 100 Singles chart at Number 16. Within three weeks it would be the Number 1 song in the nation as well. On May 26th 'MMMBop' was released in the UK and shot quickly up the charts to the Number 1 spot for three weeks. By June, 'MMMBop' was everywhere, taking Europe, Japan, Canada, Australia, and Southeast Asia by storm. Millions and millions of people worldwide could not turn on their radios or televisions without hearing 'MMMBop'.

But it would take a simple promotional visit to a shopping mall in Paramus, New Jersey, to give Hanson their first real taste of Hansonmania. Or as Taylor aptly puts it, "Our first glimpse of absolute insanity." The story goes like this: To help kick-off the official release of the *Middle of*

We weren't expecting too much, maybe a couple hundred people...but the parking lot was totally packed.

Nowhere album in early May, Hanson had flown to New York for a whirlwind week of major magazine interviews, photo sessions, and television appearances.

In the midst of all the chaos, while the guys were grabbing a few hours of practice in a rented rehearsal hall, they were asked by Mercury radio promotions executive Steve Ellis to make an extra appearance at Paramus Park Mall in New Jersey, an idea that was being proposed by a local radio station.

The idea was simple. The guys would sing a few acoustic numbers on a little stage that had been set up in front of the mall's food court. Afterwards, they would participate in a quick question and answer session with audience members. Then everyone would go home. It was that simple.

Ike, Taylor and Zac agreed to go through with the appearance albeit a bit begrudgingly. "We were rehearsing for the David Letterman Show," explains Taylor. "We were in one of our really busy streaks right then and we needed some practice for several shows."

"Yeah, (Ellis) was saying 'You guys need to do this,'" explains Ike, "and we're going 'Aw, come on we need more practice.' We had to drive 45 minutes each way to get there. It was going to end up taking 3 hours out of our day." In the end, Ellis convinced them to go. Hanson piled into their rented van and headed across the Hudson River so they could entertain what they thought would be a small number of New Jersey radio listeners who wanted to see "that 'MMMBop' band."

"We weren't expecting too much," says Taylor of the appearance. "Maybe a couple hundred people, 500 at most then, once we pulled into the parking lot, we realized the mall was just packed. It was 8:30pm, and the mall closed at nine, but the parking lot was totally packed."

"And we joked around," laughs Ike. "Oh, my gosh. Look, Sears is having a sale."

"Yeah, we were saying 'Oh, maybe everyone's here to see us,' completely kidding, of course, not expecting that at all," says Taylor.

"But when we pulled up to the mall entrance," continues Ike, "these representatives from the mall came out to the van. Their eyes were wide. They said 'We have a situation here.'" "Yeah," says Taylor as if he still can't believe it himself. "Their eyes were two inches wide, and they said, 'There're thousands of people in there.' And we're going, ' What do you mean?'"

"It was just an overwhelming experience. We really didn't have any kind of barricade around the stage at all and the stage itself was maybe a foot tall. There were people three feet away from us and all around us, everywhere, and we could see all of them singing." Ike

What they meant was this: what was supposed to be a little promotion at a local mall that would attract a few hundred fans had become an event. Instead of drawing a couple of hundred curious onlookers, the band was greeted by a crowd of more than 6,000 chanting, stomping, Hanson fanatics who had somehow managed to squeeze themselves, sardine-like, into the Paramus Park Mall.

"We were totally unprepared for that," admits Steve Greenberg. "There were over 6,000 hysterical, screaming people in there. It was just unbelievable."

The size of Hanson's success still hadn't sunk into the guys' heads, however. Even after they'd been escorted to a rear entrance of the mall and hustled "backstage," (an idea that still amuses Ike to this day, "We were backstage at a mall," he chuckles) the Hanson party continued to joke around, completely relaxed. They hadn't yet seen the crowd, after all, and they certainly hadn't heard the screams. None of them had any idea what awaited them.

"We were standing there not expecting anything," says Taylor, "and then a few security

guards came in ."

"And the minute they opened the door we heard these screams and people chanting, 'Hanson! Hanson! Hanson!'" says Ike. "When we heard it, we all stopped and looked around at each other in disbelief because we could tell the mass of people out there was incredible."

The problem was this: the guys had to somehow get from their protected "backstage" area to a tiny stage, twenty yards away, through a wall of people.

It proved to be quite a challenge. Protected by only a few security guards, plus a small following of family, friends and record executives, Hanson pressed their way through throngs of hysterical fans. It seemed like an eternity, trying to get to the tiny stage, enduring noise that's best compared to the sound of jet engines revving up for take-off. It was a life-changing experience for the guys.

"We just couldn't believe it," says Taylor. "The

"We heard screams and people chanting 'Hanson'!"

Ike

"We would plug our ears and even then the shrieks would cut through." Taylor

crowd volume was just so huge."

"The screaming was so deafening," says Ike. "There were all these arms reaching in at us, but we didn't have even close to enough security to keep anyone back. Our dad, Steve Greenberg, and all these people were trying to get themselves through the crowd to keep us from falling over and getting totally mauled. Then when we got to the stage, we began to realize the mass of people there. All of the sudden the screaming swelled."

The crowd had been waiting hours for Hanson to arrive and now that the three brothers were onstage, they went berserk. "We would plug our ears and even then the shrieks would cut through," says Taylor. "We were just trying to find a way to block out the pain."

Gazing out over the sea of people – both floors of the mall were completely impassable, with people climbing the large indoor trees planted by the escalators and standing in the decorative fountains – Isaac, Taylor and Zac tried their best to perform 'MMMBop' and 'Madeline' through a really small sound system. Armed only with Isaac's acoustic guitar, Taylor's tambourine, and Zac's shakers, Hanson lost the battle of sound with their fans. The audience, singing along with the songs, was louder than the band.

"It was an overwhelming experience," says Ike. "We really didn't have any kind of barricade around the stage at all and the stage itself was maybe a foot tall. There were people three feet away from us and all around us. They were everywhere and we could see all of them singing." Near the end of the show, Taylor made the mistake of trying to touch the hand of a fan that was reaching up to him from the crowd. Immediately, a throng of people swelled forward to cash in on the chance to touch a

rising star, and Taylor was nearly swallowed up by the crowd. He didn't make the same mistake twice.

The decision was made to scrap the question and answer portion of the appearance due in part to the lack of a proper sound system to handle the crowd noise and also for the safety of the guys. There weren't enough security guards for such an event, and the crowd was barely being held at bay as it was. It was time to get Hanson out of there.

While pushing their way out of the food court, Ike managed to pair up with the head of security and escape without a scratch. Taylor wasn't quite so lucky, however as his shirt was ripped by adoring fans, and, oddly, one of his shoelaces was ripped off his shoe. The real scare was Zac, who was almost overtaken by the crowd of fans. "He was left behind in all of the  commotion," says Taylor. "The crowd was swelling behind us and he tripped on the stairs. All these people were coming up behind him, and then our production manager swooped him up as the crowd was swelling around him. So, first of all, Zac was scared to death of the crowd, then he didn't know who was grabbing him. Afterwards he was just in shock. We were all in shock.' It was this craziness that we didn't expect."

"It was incredible," recalls Ike fondly, "As we were leaving the parking lot it sounded like hail because the crowd was banging on the van. That was pretty cool."

As it turned out, that first week of May 1997,

was a very important time for Ike, Taylor, and Zac. The Paramus Park incident was just the icing on the cake. In one unbelievable week, the guys had not only wowed American daytime talk show queen Rosie O'Donnell, MTV goddess Jenny McCarthy, and a slew of network news hosts, but also had conquered the ever hip David Letterman with an energetic performance of 'MMMBop.' That was the kick-off week for *Middle of Nowhere* and for Hanson. At the time it seemed things couldn't get busier. But there were many more crazy weeks to come.

At the end of Hanson's *Middle of Nowhere* kick-

Rolling Stone declared that 'MMMBop' will "stick in your brain like Trident in your shag carpet."

The New York Post raved that the songs are as "authentic as the teen tunes by Phil and Don Everly and as heartfelt and pure as the love songs of Ritchie Valens."

The Guardian advised it was "the freshest and funkiest thing you've heard."

Smash Hits descibed it as a musical selection box of pop chocs with all the centres you like best."

There were also the countless and inevitable

"Zac was left behind in all the commotion. The crowd was swelling behind us..." Taylor

off week in New York, they flew across the Atlantic Ocean for a whirlwind promotional tour, doing dozens of interviews with European magazines, newspapers, radio, and television stations over the course of three weeks. All the seemingly endless hours of promotion and live musical appearances across the globe paid off for Hanson, however. By the time *Middle of Nowhere* hit the shops in the late spring of 1997, 'MMMBop' fans from around the world were waiting to snatch it up. *Middle of Nowhere* entered the American charts at Number 9, selling more than 72,000 copies in its first week in the stores. Within two months, it had reached Number 2. And in the UK it shot to the top of the charts too selling over 600,000 copies.

Numerous critical accolades were ladled upon the album:

comparisons to those teen groups of twenty years ago: The Jackson 5 and The Osmonds. The constant comparisons don't seem to bother Isaac, Taylor, or Zac.

"I think we get compared to The Jackson 5 the most of any group," says Ike.

"Yeah, that was some of the first music we really listened to," adds Zac.

"And it influenced us in a large way," continues Ike. "I think it shows in our music, too. There's a soulful element to it. I think it's cool when we're compared to groups like The Jackson 5 because they were amazing. I mean, they were The Jackson 5."

"They rocked," says Taylor firmly. "It's a real compliment when somebody compares us to them. But the way we've always described ourselves is that we're three guys who write, play, and sing our music, and that really pulls it

all together. That's what Hanson is."

After a brief stay at home following their European promotional tour, Hanson returned to London, England, in the spring of 1997 to film a video for their second single, "Where's The Love?" Again, they chose to work with director Tamra Davis. The video was shot over the course of three days, making use of locations at Waterloo Station, Trafalgar Square, Covent Garden, and Battersea Power Station. Primarily a performance video, 'Where's The Love?' is less about showing the guys running around, and more about putting them in cool locations, instruments in hand, and showing crowd reaction.

"It basically worked the same way as it did with the first video," says Taylor, "where we would call Tamra and tell her all our ideas about the video and she would listen to them. Then, after hearing them all she sent us a treatment, her ideas about the video, which were mainly all our ideas, twisted together with hers.

The night before we started actually filming, she met us in London and showed us slides of the locations, and we put together all the wardrobe for the shoot."

"We had been in Europe for several weeks at that point and that was the last thing that we did while we were there," says Ike. "It went very smoothly and it ended up being very, very cool." "It was really fun because the crew was awesome," says Taylor. "And the ideas that we discussed with Tamra were actually put in the video. All the sites we were picturing were almost exactly like the locations where we filmed."

After they had completed the 'Where's The Love?' shoot, Hanson flew back to the States for a series of promotional shows in Detroit, Minneapolis, Charlotte, and Oklahoma City. Crowds at the Oklahoma City venue were so large that people had to be turned away at the front gate.

After a few days' rest at home in Tulsa, Hanson was off again. This time they flew back to Los Angeles, to make an appearance on The Tonight Show with Jay Leno where they performed 'Where's The Love?' to an appreciative audience of screaming fans. Leno then invited Hanson over to his guest couch for a chat. "Leno is a really nice guy," says Ike. "He stopped by the dressing room before the show just to say 'Hello'." "He's very down to earth," agrees Taylor. Directly after that appearance, the band boarded a plane for yet another promotional tour – this time to Japan, Southeast Asia, and Australia. The Far East was about to meet Hanson face to face.

"The video was all of our ideas, twisted together." Taylor

Hanson spent the next few weeks in Japan where they were greeted with crowds of enthusiastic fans and Japanese hospitality. The Japanese – long known for their love of pop music – had immediately fallen for the irresistible bounce of "MMMBop," upon its release, rocketing the song into the top ten. By the time Hanson arrived in Tokyo, they were already somewhat of a national sensation.

Hanson spent much of their time in an endless stream of interviews and press conferences as well as making lots of television appearances. During one interview at a Tokyo radio station, such a large throng of fans had gathered outside hoping to catch a glimpse of the guys that station officials decided it would be in their best interests to appease the crowd. Fans were escorted, 20 to 25 at a time, through the

station where they were able to see Isaac, Taylor and Zachary for a few seconds through a control room window as they were being interviewed. Everywhere they went in Japan, Hanson received a warm welcome from their fans.

Hanson's experiences with wildly devoted Japanese fans were a good warm-up for the response they got when they moved on to the next leg of their tour: Australia.

The band began by spending some time in

Sydney – concentrating on their usual promotional duties, which included a very unusual performance for a group of radio contest winners on a ferry in Sydney Harbor.

"It was kind of an awkward thing," says Taylor, "because we were in the hull of this boat that was packed with a crowd of contest winners. "But in that situation it seemed like there were

"It's not very often you're on a rocking boat singing to a packed room of girls, after all. It was pretty wild." Taylor

a whole lot more because it was such a small area," continues Taylor. "Not to mention the video cameras and press. It was a very unique situation for performing. It's not very often you're on a rocking boat singing to a packed room of girls, after all. It was pretty wild."

Ike agrees. "They were definitely very enthusiastic. Before we came down to do the show, all of the crowd were singing 'MMMBop' word for word. I mean they knew every single word."

"Before Australia, we'd been doing a lot more concert situations where we were not very close to the audience. But this was different because it was very, very intimate so it was a lot of fun."

After they were finished in Sydney, Hanson got on a flight to Melbourne, Australia's second largest city, to complete the Australian leg of their tour. It was at the Melbourne airport that things began to get a bit crazy. Crowds of hysterical fans had descended on the airport to greet their musical heroes.

"After we landed," says Taylor, "the flight attendant said 'You guys need to wait until everybody else gets off the plane. You need to be the last ones off.' We couldn't figure it out and asked, 'Why?' They just smiled and said, 'Just wait.' So we waited, and we were the last ones off, and just before we got inside the terminal they said, 'I hope you're ready 'cause there's a lot of people out there.'"

They weren't kidding either. Hundreds of screaming girls were clogging up the terminal. "When we went out into the waiting area it was just totally wacko," grins Taylor. "I mean, in Japan there were a lot of people at the airport, but it was very much under control."Not here, however.

"There was a circle around us," laughs Zac, "and there were a thousand fans there, and we were thinking, 'Help us!'"

The guys had to push their way through the mob with only minimal security, bringing to mind vivid scenes of their Paramus Park Mall experience. "There was a chain of four or five security guards around us but that didn't stop them. The fans were just jumping on them and putting their arms through and screaming" says Taylor.

The hysteria of their Australian fans was caused by the fact that 'MMMBop' had been Number 1 in Australia for nine weeks by the time the boys arrived there. Combined with a big "Hanson is Coming!" promotional push, this national love

of the band had reached a fever pitch by July... as evidenced by another unusual mall appearance.

"At first, it was supposed to be an in-store performance," explains Taylor. "Very small, not a big deal. But in Australia we had a very big following, so the organizers had to move the appearance into this huge parking garage because they were expecting a lot of people."

"The night before, we went down to the garage," says Zac. "We were thinking, 'We'll never fill this place. This is huge.'"

"It was winter in Australia so Melbourne was really cold," says Taylor. "We let a few fans in when we did the sound check that night because they were camping overnight outside the mall so they could get good seats. The mall decided to let them in to sleep inside instead of sleeping in the car garage because it was so cold."

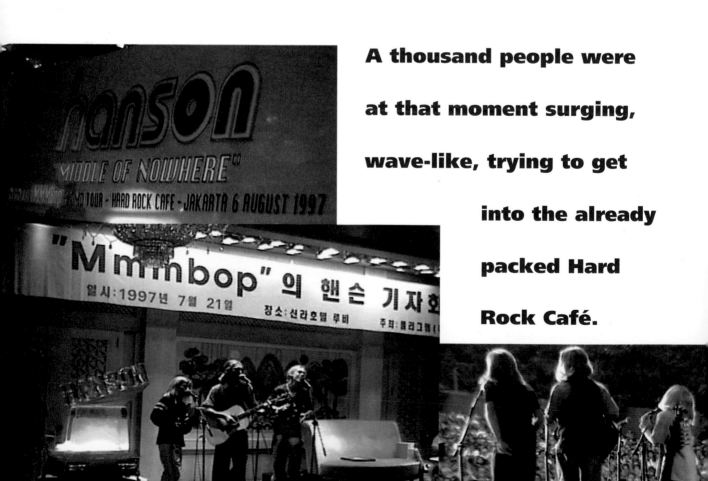

A thousand people were at that moment surging, wave-like, trying to get into the already packed Hard Rock Café.

'People were grabbing parts of our clothing, they were grabbing our hair and pulling it'

The band's concerns about their ability to fill the parking garage were unnecessary, as it turned out. The next day, more than 20,000 fans arrived to see them.

"It was amazing," says Taylor. "People flew in from all across Australia and Tasmania to see us. This parking garage went so far back that you couldn't see the end of the people. It was definitely our biggest show so far." Or as Zac so elegantly puts it: "Yeah, it was, I mean, it was just...wow."

The sight of 20,000 screaming Australian fans in a mall parking garage was an awesome experience Hanson won't forget, however, another wild experience was in store for them at the next stop on their promotional tour: Jakarta, the capital of Indonesia. This city of 6 million people is situated on the island of Java and is home to perhaps the most frenzied Hanson fans on planet Earth.

It all began with yet another promotional appearance that was supposed to consist of a press conference followed by three acoustic songs. The place: The Hard Rock Café, Jakarta. The idea: The guys would answer questions from the press for a while, then a limited number of fans would be allowed into the restaurant to sit in the balcony and watch Hanson's brief acoustic set. The problem: thousands wanted to get in.

"We did the press conference," says Zac, "and then they let some fans in and we started our first song. Then, all of a sudden, near the end of the song we see this surge of people coming from the back of the restaurant."

"All the press people started scrambling, grabbing their notes, going 'Oh, my God!'" adds Taylor. "Our security guard was shouting, 'Guys! Guys! Get off stage,'" says Ike. "So, we stopped the song halfway through and got off stage."

A wise move considering a thousand people were at that moment surging, wave-like, trying to get into the already packed Hard Rock Café. Somehow, the doors that were to have remained bolted to the public had been thrown wide open, allowing a tidal wave of human bodies to sweep into the building.

"I hope you're ready 'cause there's a lot of people out there."

"We tried to calm everybody down," recalls Taylor, "because there were people on a balcony and they were just hanging over the edge. It would have been so easy for someone just to fall off." "Or for them to knock the railing over," suggests Ike. "People were just pushing and shoving," continues Taylor. "I mean, photographers were going down on the floor. The press was not exactly ready for it."

"The press was trying to be security," chuckles Zac. "Actually, the press was just kind of getting pushed around," counters Ike. Zac picks up the story. "After that we came back on stage and did the other two songs, but immediately after we'd finished a security guy said, 'You guys have got to go.' So we jumped off the stage." The situation was beginning to get out of

control, with still more people trying to cram their way into the restaurant and those inside becoming increasingly unruly. Unfortunately, the only way out was directly through the throng. "We got through the huge crowd of fans, through the kitchen, and onto the roof," says Ike. "As we were going across the roof we turned around and there were about 50 fans chasing us. They saw us and started screaming. A few record label guys ran back to stop them so we could keep going."

"Then we had to go through another restaurant, and as we went through everyone started noticing it was us and then they started hurling themselves at us," says Zac, amazed. "People were grabbing parts of our clothing," says Ike. "They were grabbing our hair and pulling it, and jumping on us and almost ripping off our clothes."

"They were the most aggressive fans definitely," says Taylor. "Once we got in our bus – which was quite a feat – they surrounded us and they started beating on the bus. All you heard was boomboomboomboom as they pounded on the sides of the van and the windows."

Back at the Hard Rock, the crowd who hadn't been able to push their way inside began throwing stones at the club. They refused to believe the news that Hanson had already left, and were growing more impatient by the second. Thinking quickly, the Hard Rock management averted a potentially nasty situation by providing the crowd with the next best thing to Hanson in person.

"They played a video tape of the songs we had just done and we were told that everybody started crying and taking pictures of the video screen" says Zac. "Definitely an experience to remember."